How do You Know the Bible is from GOD?

Kyle Butt M.A.

**Great Oaks
Children's Library**

How do You Know the Bible is from God?

ISBN: 0-932859-65-8

Library of Congress: 2004107302

Cover artwork by J. William Myers

Concept and interior design by Charles McCown

Printed in China

Apologetics Press
230 Landmark Drive
Montgomery, Alabama
36117-2752
www.ApologeticsPress.org

Dedication

To Sheila Keckler Butt, my mother and my friend —whose passion for teaching the Truth has not ceased.

Chapter 1
The Special Book

Television, video games, and computers are very exciting things that capture the attention of young men and women all over the world. Through them, we are able to visit far-off places, fight deadly dragons, race fast cars, and

go on a million other wild adventures. But when the TV is turned off, the video games are put away, and the computer is shut down, we realize that we never actually left our rooms, the fast cars never really moved, and the dragons weren't so deadly after all. It was just pretend, not real.

But what if I told you about a book that tells of real battles between men and giants? A book that describes a real creature with fire bellowing from its mouth and smoke steaming from its nostrils. A book that tells of seas being parted and people walking through on dry land. This book tells of the long and gruesome war between the evil forces of darkness and the all-powerful Force of good. It is alive and exciting, but the best part about this book is that it is real life. It can never be unplugged, turned off, or shut down. It shows how ordinary humans can be transformed into God's children.

Maybe you have heard of this book; in fact, you probably own one—the Bible. But do you know just how special this book is? Just in case you don't know what a treasure you have, let me tell you some wonderful things about The Book.

The Bible is God's Word

Thousands of years ago, God spoke directly to people. He did not use a book to tell them how to live; He simply spoke to them like your mother or father talks to you. Some of those men wrote down what God said to them so that their children, grandchildren, and even future generations would know the things God wanted them to do. Over the years, the writings of these men were put together in a book that we call the Bible. God used about 40 men to write the Bible—men who were very different from one another. Some of them were very rich kings, while others were just poor shepherds. Some of the men were very well educated, while others had little education at all. They wrote during different times in history. In fact, the Bible was written over a period of about 1,600 years. God instructed Moses to write the first books of the Old Testament in approximately 1,500 B.C. And the apostle John wrote Revelation (the last book of the New Testament) about A.D. 100.

Amazingly, although many of the books of the Bible were written hundreds of years apart by different men, they still fit together so that they read like one story. Of course, they fit together so well because God was behind their writing, instructing each man what to write.

Millions of People Buy It

Since the words of the Bible came from God, that makes it the most valuable book in the whole world. For this reason, people have bought more copies of the Bible than any other book in the history of the world. Since the year 1947, at least nine billion Bibles have been distributed around the world. (If one person handed out 30,000 every day, it would take him 821 years to disperse 9 billion Bibles.) The Bible has been translated into more than 800 different languages, and over 200 countries now have Bibles. The Bible is the number one best-selling book in the entire world.

The Treasure Map

If I told you I had a map that would lead you to the biggest pile of treasure in the world, would you want to see that map? Of course you would. Well, that is exactly what the Bible is—a treasure map that leads to the most wonderful riches imaginable. God knows how humans need to live in order to be happy in this life and in order to go to heaven when they die. He put those directions into the Bible. When a person reads and follows the Bible, it is like they are following the most valuable treasure map of all time. It is no wonder that so many people want to get their hands on this remarkable book!

How Did We Get the Bible?

If a friend asked how you got your Bible, you might tell him it was given to you for your birthday, or that you bought it in a bookstore. But how do you know that the Bible you bought is the "real thing"? How do you know that it is filled with the words that God instructed those 40 holy men to write thousands of years ago? After all, the Bible is a very old book. How do we know that it has not been changed over the many hundreds of years since it was written? Is there proof that the books of the Bible we have in the 21st century are the same as the ones people had 500 or 1,000 years ago? What if the Bible that we have today is not really God's Word?

After reading this book about where the Bible came from, you will be able to answer

all these questions, and many more. What you will find as you learn about the origin of the Holy Book is that God took extra special care of it so that as long as this Earth exists, humans will have God's Treasure Map.

Chapter 2

Ancient Writing Materials

We live in a time when writing notes, typing letters, and printing books is very easy to do. If you want to write a note to someone, all you have to do is take a piece of paper from a notebook or pad, use an ink pen, pencil, or magic marker, and write until your hand hurts. Everything you need to write is at your fingertips. Or what if you need to type a report or project? Simply find a computer that has a printer with plenty of paper, type, and press the print button. In fact, using a computer even allows you to make several copies at one time.

But how did people write letters or papers before pens, pencils, typewriters, or computers were invented? And what did they write on before paper was invented. The truth is, paper and pens as we know them have been around for only a very short time. Thousands of years ago (when the Bible was being written), it was not very easy to write or print things. So let's see how people of the past wrote.

Please Take Out One Clean Piece of Stone and a Number 2 Chisel

Can you imagine a schoolteacher asking her class to take out a clean piece of stone in order to take a spelling test? Yet, as silly as that sounds to us, flat slabs of rock probably were some of the first

5

things used as "paper." To write on these rock slabs, people used a sharp piece of metal or hard rocks. They would engrave the words deep into the tablets of stone. Writing on stone took many hours to accomplish, but when you think about it, it is easy to see why ancient people would use this form of writing. After all, how difficult is it to find rocks? And what material could be better for keeping records that would last a long, long time? Words carved into stone could not be erased easily. There were no backspace buttons or spell checkers involved in stone writing.

Moses used stone tablets for the Ten Commandments. We read in Exodus 34: 1: "And the Lord said to Moses, 'Cut two tablets of stone like the first ones, and I will write on these tablets the words that were on the first tablets.' " Writing on stone was a way to ensure that the words were preserved for many generations.

But you can imagine some of the problems that might come with carving in stone. What if you had lots of pages to write? It would be difficult to carry a 30 "page" book of stone. Also, if you accidentally slipped while you were writing, no erasers could remove the mistakes. Plus, carving stone took a long time. Because of this, the ancient people kept looking for other ways to write.

Common Clay

Clay was another material ancient writers used. Clay had many qualities that made it a good writing material. For one, it was common and inexpensive. Also, it was easy to write on. When clay is moist, it is soft and can be engraved easily using a stone or stick. Once the clay dries, the words engraved in it become permanently set. Ezekiel mentioned a clay tablet in chapter 4:1 of his book in the Old Testa-

Credit: The Schøyen Collection MS 1717

ment. And many clay tablets—thousands of years old—have been found buried in the ground.

Although clay could be written on easily, it had a few problems. Have you ever dropped a red clay pot like the ones in which people keep flowers? If you have, you know that clay breaks very easily. Imagine working hard on a clay writing tablet all day and then accidentally dropping and breaking it. Another problem with clay was that it was difficult to carry a lot of it at one time (just like stone). So the ancients continued to look for other materials.

Popular Papyrus

Near shallow lakes and rivers grew a tall reed called papyrus. It especially grew by the Nile River in Egypt. The ancient people would harvest this hollow reed, slit it down the middle, and roll it out flat. Then they would take these reeds and glue them together. After gluing many of the reeds together, a rock was needed to smooth the surface of the papyrus so that people could write on it just like paper. The ink, made from plants or dyes, would be ap-

Old, worn-out page of a papyrus document

plied to the finished sheet using a sharp stick, quill, or other "pen-like" instrument.

Papyrus was one of the most popular ways to write and send messages. The sheets were glued into long pieces that were rolled into scrolls. The scrolls mentioned in Revelation 5:1 were most likely papyrus. The apostles and other New Testament writers probably used papyrus to write their original books.

With the use of papyrus, lots of information could be carried at one time (unlike the use of clay and stone). Also, if a person dropped a papyrus scroll, it did not crack and break. Writing on papyrus was not difficult either; it did not take hours to engrave and dry. Papyrus was similar to our paper; in fact, our word paper comes from the word papyrus (do you see the similarities?).

With all the advantages that came with the use of papyrus, some disadvantages tagged along. One big problem was that papyrus decayed easily and did not last very long. Much like paper, if it fell into water or if it was exposed to rain, it would decay. The way that ancient people fixed this problem was to copy the information on the old sheets of papyrus to freshly pressed sheets. For this reason, many copies of documents (especially the New Testament) have been found on papyrus.

Credit: The Schøyen Collection MS 1644/1

Lovely Leather

Parchment and vellum are the names given to animal skins that were used as "paper." These animal skins would be dried and polished with a stone. Many times the ancient writers dyed the skins purple and used gold ink to write on them.

of writing materials. The next time we pick up a sheet of paper and ballpoint pen or sit down to type on a computer, let's be thankful for the great progress that our ancestors made in the area of writing. And let's be thankful that the ancient people had ways to preserve the Word of God so that it could come to us in our modern day and age.

Leather was lightweight, did not decay as quickly as papyrus, and could be produced by anyone in the world (not just people who lived by lakes or rivers). For these reasons, parchment and vellum became popular. Well-preserved copies of the Bible dating from about A.D. 200 have been found written on leather.

Thank You, Ancestors

Many other materials were used to write, record, and document the past. Wood, ivory, bone, and shells are a few. But the ones mentioned earlier in this chapter were the most popular forms

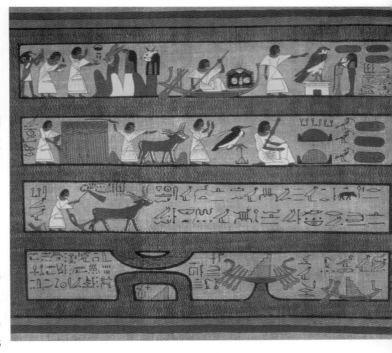

Egyptian fragment of the Book of the Dead

Chapter 3

Did the Bible Come from God?

Suppose you took a piece of notebook paper and colored it green with a magic marker. Then you used a black marker to write the number 100 in all four corners of the paper. Do you think that you could use that piece of "money" to buy candy at the nearest gas station? Of course you couldn't. But why couldn't you? The reason your fake money would not work is because it did not come from the United States government. Since **you** made the "money" instead of the government, then it isn't worth anything. But if you had a piece of money that was created by the government, then it could be used to buy things.

In a way, the Bible is like that. If human beings, who lived many years ago, simply made up the things in the Bible, then it does not have any more power than a book of fairytales. But if the Bible came from God, and if He put all the ideas and thoughts in it, then it has the power to tell people how they should live. **Did** the Bible come from God? And, if it did, how did He get it to humans?

God Inspired the Bible

Many times during Bible class or the preacher's sermon, you might hear a person say that God "inspired" men to write the Bible. But what does "inspire" mean? The word inspire comes from the Latin word *inspirare*. It means "to breathe upon or into." If we say that the Bible is inspired, we simply mean that God breathed His Word into its writers; He gave them the message He wanted them to write. This guaranteed that the writers of Holy Scripture did not make any mistakes. When a person says that the Bible is the "Word of God," that does not mean that God sat down at a desk with a pen and paper and wrote it out Himself. It just means that God breathed into the holy men what He wanted them to write.

In Exodus 19, the Bible tells how Moses went up to Mt. Sinai and received commandments from God, while the Israelites waited below the mountain.

But how do we know that the Bible is inspired by God? What makes the Bible any different from all the other books in the world?

The Bible Claims to Be Inspired by God

Many verses in the Bible claim that it is the Word of God. One of the most well-known passages is 2 Timothy 3:16-17: "All Scripture is given by inspiration of God, and is profitable for doctrine, for reproof, for correction, for instruction in righteousness, that the man of God may be complete, thoroughly equipped for every good work." In these verses, the apostle Paul explained to the young preacher Timothy that the Bible is the most valuable book known to man, because it is God-breathed.

Another passage where the Bible claims to be inspired is 2 Peter 1:20-21: "Knowing this first, that no prophecy of Scripture is of any private interpretation, for prophecy never came by the will of man, but holy men of God spoke as they were moved by the Holy Spirit."

In fact, over 2,700 times the Bible says something similar to "the Lord said" or "the Word of the Lord." That is truly amazing, considering that many Bibles only have about 1,300 pages. On average, the Bible claims that it is God's Word a little over two times per page.

Of course, just because the Bible claims to be the Word of God

does not make it so. I can claim to be the President of the United States, but that does not make me President. In order to prove that the Bible is inspired by God, it must be shown that it contains things no other book in the world contains.

Amazing Facts about the Bible

First, the writing of the Bible is truly remarkable. It was written over a period of about 1,600 years by approximately 40 different writers who were from a variety of different backgrounds and education levels. Some were fishermen or farmers, some were educated scribes, and some were kings. Yet when we look at this book (written by such different men over so many years), it shows an amazing unity —as if a single, guiding hand was behind it.

The Old Testament starts with the beginning of the Universe, and ends in Malachi with the promise of a coming Messiah. The New Testament starts with the birth of the Messiah in Matthew, and ends in Revelation with the destruction of the Universe and the promise of heaven. Every book in the Bible connects to the other books perfectly to tell the story of man's sin and God's plan of salvation.

Miraculous Knowledge

Second, the unity of the Bible is remarkable, but there are many other areas that show the Bible to be beyond the abilities of mere human authors to produce. The Bible presents astonishing facts that the writers, on their own, simply could not have known.

In Genesis 6:15, God instructed Noah to build an ark that was 300 cubits long, 50 cubits wide, and 30 cubits high. This is a ratio of 30 to 5 to 3 (length to width to height). The ark was one of the largest floating ships ever created. In terms that we understand better, the ark was about 450 feet long, 75 feet wide, and 45 feet high. In 1844, a man named Isambard K. Brunnel built his giant ship, the *Great Britain*. He used almost the exact same ratio of the ark—30:5:3.

As it turns out, these measurements are perfect for a huge boat built to stay afloat rather than for speed. Obviously the ark was not built for speed, since it had nowhere to go! What is more, shipbuilders during World War II used a similar ratio to build the *SS Jeremiah O'Brien*, which eventually was nicknamed "the ugly duckling"—a barge-like boat built to carry huge amounts of cargo, and one that had basically the same ratio as the ark. How did

The *SS Jeremiah O'Brien* enters the English Channel—May 21, 1994. Photo by Royal Navy

Noah know the perfect ratio to use in building the ark? Brunnel and others like him had many generations of shipbuilding knowledge to use, but Noah's boat was the first of its kind. Where did he get such information? From the Master Builder! We should thank God for inspiring the Bible, because He talks to us through its pages.

Questions and Activities Chapters 1-3

Vocabulary

Papyrus   Vellum
Inspired   Cubit
Parchment   Scroll

Review

1. About how many men did God use to write the Bible?
2. How many years did it take to write the entire Bible?
3. What evidence found in chapter one of this book shows that the Bible is a very popular book?
4. Name at least four ancient writing materials.
5. What material usually was used to make scrolls?
6. What were some advantages and disadvantages of using stone?
7. How was papyrus made?
8. How many times does the Bible claim to be the Word of God?
9. List some Bible verses which say that the Bible is inspired by God.
10. What was the ratio (length to width to height) of Noah's ark?

Critical Thinking

Name the ancient writing material that would fit each clue (some clues may have more than one answer).

1. Very heavy
2. Breaks very easily
3. Would burn quickly
4. Light weight
5. Difficult to erase
6. Would fall apart if left outside
7. Easy to erase when wet
8. Comes from an animal
9. Could write on it using a quill
10. Lasted a long time

Miniature Ark

Using Popsicle™ sticks and wood glue, construct an ark that is 30 centimeters long, 5 centimeters wide, and 3 centimeters high. Then cover the inside with Silly Putty™. Fill up a large container with water, and watch your miniature ark float.

Chapter 4
The Bible Predicts the Future

The last chapter discussed how God inspired the Bible. He breathed His Word into ancient men, and told them exactly what He wanted them to write. Some people try to say that God did not inspire the Bible. These people say that the Bible is a good book, but it did not come from God. But that cannot be true, because the Bible does things that no other book in the world can do. One thing that the Bible does that other books can't do is that it tells the future. No other book in the world tells the future like the Bible does.

The Bible Predicts the Future

In Ezekiel 26:1-14, the Bible tells about a city named Tyre. This city was very wealthy and secure when Ezekiel wrote about it. Yet, the holy prophet Ezekiel predicted that the city would be destroyed. Many people did not believe Ezekiel because the city looked like it was too powerful to be destroyed. But the prophet told many detailed things that would happen to the city. First, he said that a king from Babylon by the name of Nebuchadnezzar would fight against the city. After that, many nations would come up to fight Tyre, and the city would be leveled and scraped clean like a bare rock. Ezekiel also predicted that the city's stones, logs, and soil would be thrown into the sea. The area around the city would become a place for the spreading of fishermen's nets. And,

This photograph shows the land bridge that was built by the enemies of Tyre.

years. Then, in 332 B.C., Alexander the Great conquered the city—but not with ease. To get to the island, he had his army literally "scrape clean" the inland city of all logs, stones, and dirt. He then dumped those materials into the ocean, creating a "land bridge" to the island.

finally, the city would never be rebuilt to its former glory.

What is amazing about this story is that Ezekiel was exactly right about everything he said. History records that each one of these predictions came true. Nebuchadnezzar, the king of Babylon, surrounded the city of Tyre and broke through the strong walls. But when he finally was able to take the city in about 573 B.C., his victory was empty. He did not know that the people of Tyre had left the city and moved to a little island just off the coast. That island remained safe for about the next 241

The "great" city never regained its position of wealth and power. The prophet Ezekiel looked hundreds of years into the future and predicted that the city of Tyre would be a bald rock where fishermen gathered to open their nets. And that is exactly what happened.

The Coming Christ

In addition to its prophecies dealing with people, places, and events, the Old Testament contains more than 300 prophecies about Jesus. These prophecies are called "messianic" prophecies because they tell about the coming "Messiah" or

Savior. These prophecies were written to tell the world about the One Who would come to save humankind from sin.

Psalm 22:16-18 is a great example of a messianic prophecy. David wrote Psalm 22 in approximately 1000 B.C. In that psalm, he described exactly what would happen to the Christ Who was supposed to come and save the world. David said that sinful people were going to pierce the hands and feet of the Messiah. He also explained that those same peo-ple were going to "cast lots" (like rolling dice) for the clothing of Christ.

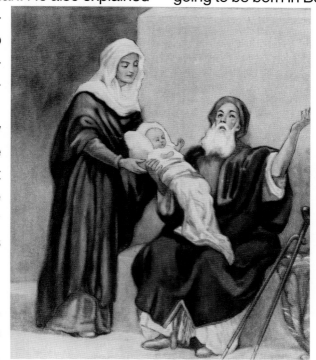

David's prophecy is amazing because it came true almost 1,000 years after he wrote it. In Matthew 27:35, the Bible tells us that Christ was crucified. When a person was crucified, big nails were driven in his hands and feet.

Also, soldiers who hung Jesus on the cross "cast lots" for His clothing. How did David know that Jesus' hands and feet would be pierced, and that soldiers would cast lots for His clothing? David could have known such small details about the future only if God inspired him to write the psalm.

Another amazing prophecy about Jesus is found in Micah 5:2, where the prophet predicted that the Savior of the world was going to be born in Bethlehem. In Matthew 2:1, the Bible tells us that Bethlehem was the city where Jesus was born. How could Micah have known, hundreds of years before it took place, that Jesus was to be born in Bethlehem? God must have told him what to write.

No one but the true God can tell the future and be correct every time. Others have tried, but they

have failed. The Bible explains how important being able to tell the future is: "When the word of the prophet comes to pass, the prophet will be known as one whom the Lord has truly sent" (Jeremiah 28:9). If someone or something (like a book) can predict the future and be right 100% of the time, then that person or book was sent directly from God. The Bible tells the future. And that means that only God could have sent it.

Chapter 5—How Did We Get the Old Testament?

Moses began to write the first books of the Old Testament almost 3,500 years ago. All of the original documents that Moses, Isaiah, Jeremiah, and the other Old Testament writers produced have been destroyed. We have only copies of their writings. So, how do we know that the original books were copied correctly? Can we be sure that the book of Genesis that we read in the 21st century is the same book that God inspired Moses to write 3,500 years ago? Yes, we can be sure that the Old Testament that we read today has been copied accurately. Let's look at the reasons why.

Serious Scribes

Sometimes kids get in trouble at school, and for punishment they are made to copy pages out of the dictionary or encyclopedia. Copying such pages is boring. But suppose you lived in a time when the printing press or the computer did not exist. If each school needed a dictionary, how would so many copies be produced? Well, someone would have to sit down and copy the original by hand. Such a person was called a scribe. Scribes copied almost any type of document imaginable—business receipts, legal documents, marriage certificates, and more.

Scribes took their jobs very seriously because the slightest mistake could make

An inkwell (far left) found close to the Dead Sea Scolls. The pointed instrument next to it was a pen or stylus from the same area.

a big difference. For instance, suppose that a person bought a piece of land for 20 gold pieces. If the scribe did not pay close attention to his work, he might write 2 gold pieces or 200 gold pieces, drastically altering the original price.

But there was one group of scribes who took their jobs more seriously than all the rest. Those ancient scribes who copied the Old Testament went to great lengths to make sure they made no mistakes. They knew that they were copying the Word of God, and they wanted to be absolutely sure that it was done right. For this reason, they made many rules concerning copies of the Old Testament. These rules included using a special kind of ink,

making sure that each letter of a word was spaced exactly a hairsbreadth (the thickness of one hair) from its neighbor, and never writing even the smallest letter from memory.

One group of scribes, who were known as the Masoretes, made even stricter rules than the ones above. They counted every single verse, word, and letter of the Old Testament books that they copied. They also counted how many times a letter was used and which verse, word, and letter should be exactly in the middle of the book. The Masoretes were some of the world's greatest perfectionists.

Where did All the Copies Go?

The ancient Jewish scribes made thousands of copies of the Old Testament. With so many scribes working on the Old Testament, it would seem that we should find thousands of ancient copies. But that is not exactly the case. Although we do find many copies of the Old Testament, thousands of the copies that were produced have been lost. What happened to all the copies?

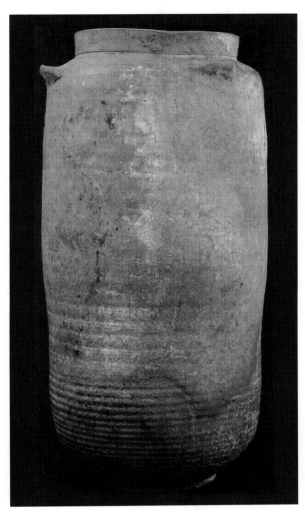

About 40 jars like this one were found among the caves near the Dead Sea. Scribes filled these jars with scrolls. The jars kept the scrolls from getting wet. Many ancient scrolls have been found because they were stored well.

Credit: The Schøyen Collection MS 1655/1

The scribes were very particular about their copies of the Old Testament books. If one of their copies began to get older, or its pages began to fade, they would take it and bury it in the ground or burn it. They did not want to take the chance of the faded copy being misread or recopied incorrectly. Furthermore, the scribes greatly respected the name of God. Any document that had God's name written on it was viewed as holy, and had to be kept in good shape. Once a holy document became old or worn, it was given a proper burial. For these reasons, many of the copies of the Old Testament no longer exist.

Is It Too Late?

Even though the scribes took great care to copy the Old Testament faithfully, some people still questioned its accuracy. The reason for this was that the earliest copies of the entire Old Testament that were available were copied in A.D. 900 and later (that is almost 2,500 years after some of the original documents were written). With such a long span of time, how could anyone know if the text had remained correct?

The Dead Sea Scrolls

In 1948, the way that the world viewed the Old Testament changed forever. An Arab boy was looking for a lost goat. He threw a rock into a small cave and heard a sound like breaking pottery. Curious about the sound, he went into the cave and found some leather scrolls with ancient writing on them. It turns out that hundreds of scrolls were hidden in these caves around the Dead Sea. The scrolls most likely were written by a group of people known as the Essenes.

The white arrow points to one of the caves where the Dead Sea Scrolls were discovered.

But the most important things that were discovered in the caves were copies of many of the books of the Old Testament. These copies were produced from about 200 B.C. to A.D. 100, making them almost 900 years older than the oldest available copies of the Old Testament.

One scroll found in the Dead Sea caves was of particular importance. It was a scroll of the book of Isaiah (only a few parts were missing). What was amazing about this scroll was that when it was compared to the text of Isaiah produced 900 years after it, they matched almost word for word. Only a few small variations existed. The Dead Sea scrolls had proven to the world that the Old Testament had been copied faithfully and passed down to the current time. Once again, the world witnessed that God had made sure that His Word was accurately passed from one generation to the next!

Chapter 6

How Did We Get the New Testament?

Almost 1,900 years ago, God inspired the writers of the New Testament to pen their books and letters. The actual letters and books written by these men were known as "autographs." Unfortunately, we do not have any of the original documents that these men wrote. Why didn't God preserve these original documents so that we could see and possibly touch them? We cannot be sure of why God did not preserve the original documents. Maybe He knew that some people might value the actual piece of papyrus and not the words and ideas written on it. Or maybe He knew that some people might think themselves to be more holy than others just because they had an original autograph. For whatever reasons, God did not preserve the original documents that the New Testament writers produced. So, the question arises: "How do we know that the New Testament we read in the 21st century is the same one that God inspired almost 1,900 years ago?"

Check the Time

Understanding when the original documents of the New Testament were written will help us determine how well they have been preserved. Let's take a look at when the New Testament was written. The earliest events recorded in the New Testament are those surrounding the birth of Jesus. He was born in approximately

A.D. 1 (we date our calendars from the birth of Christ). He lived almost 33 years, and then was crucified. Therefore, since the New Testament tells about His life and death, it could not have been written much earlier than A.D. 33. In fact, one book (Acts) tells about things that happened around A.D. 50-60. When, exactly, was the New Testament written? We cannot be sure of the exact date when each book was written, but we do know that the entire New Testament was written between approximately A.D. 35 and A.D. 100.

Many Manuscripts

Unlike the scribes who copied the Old Testament, people who copied the New Testament did not see the need to bury or burn old, worn-out copies of the Scriptures. For this reason, thousands of manuscripts of the New Testament exist. A "manuscript" is a hand-written copy of an old document that was copied in its original language. Since the New Testament originally was written in Greek, the manuscripts also are written in Greek. Over

This manuscript of a part of the book of Matthew dates to about A.D. 350.

Credit: The Schøyen Collection MS 2650

5,700 old manuscripts exist that contain all or part of the New Testament.

The fact that so many old copies of the New Testament exist is truly amazing, especially when it is compared to other ancient books. For instance, one of the most famous ancient books in history is *The Illiad*, which was written by the Greek writer Homer. But there are only about 700 manuscripts of his book.

What is even more amazing than the huge number of New Testament manuscripts is the time that they were produced. Some have been found that were copied only a few years after they were written. One manuscript known as the *John Ryland's Papyrus* has portions of the gospel of John written on it. It was found in Egypt, and dates back to A.D. 130—just a few years after the New Testament was completed.

Quotable Quotes

Many of you have listened to a preacher talk about the Bible. Sometimes that preacher might quote a certain Bible verse. In order to quote the verse, he had to have read it sometime before his lesson. So what does that have to do with how we got the New Testament? There were many ancient preachers who quoted the Bible just like preachers do today. These early preachers lived only a few years after the Bible was written, and they quoted from it quite often. For instance, a man named Ignatius lived around A.D. 70-110, and quoted from the books of Matthew, Acts, Romans, and several others. Another man named Polycarp lived around A.D. 70-156, and also quoted from the Bible. It often has been said that even if we did not have a single written copy of the New Testament, we could put one together from the quotes of these ancient preachers.

Now let's put the pieces together. If the ancient preachers who lived around A.D. 70-110 quoted from the New Testament, then that means that the New Testament had to be written before they quoted it. And it also means that we can compare the New Testament that we read in the 21st century to the quotes that they produced in those early years. When we compare the two, we find that many of the quotes are almost identical to the Bible passages —word for word. God used these preachers to help preserve the New Testament.

Compare the New Testament to Other Ancient Books

All of the evidence in this chapter shows that the New Testament we have is the same one that the inspired men wrote. But to make this chapter complete, we must compare the New Testament with other ancient books. How does the New Testament measure up when it is compared to these other books?

To tell the truth, the other books do not have a fraction of the evidence that the New Testament does to support its accuracy. God made sure that the Bible was passed down faithfully from one generation to the next. So the next time you read a verse out of any one of the New Testament books, you can be sure that it is the Word of God.

How Does the New Testament Measure Up to Other Ancient Books?

Title of Ancient Book	Date It was Written	Date of Earliest Manuscript	Number of Manuscripts
Homer's *Illiad*	700 B.C.	Unknown	643
History of Herodotus	425 B.C.	A.D. 900	8
Josephus' *Jewish Wars*	A.D. 70	A.D. 400	9
Histories of Tacitus	A.D. 100	A.D. 900	2
New Testament	A.D. 35-100	A.D. 125	5,735

Questions and Activities Chapters 4-6

Vocabulary

Messiah   Scribe

Masoretes   Autographs

Manuscript   Prophecy

Review

1. In Ezekiel 26, the Bible foretold the destruction of what city?
2. How did Alexander the Great get to the island off the coast of Tyre?
3. How many "messianic" prophecies are in the Old Testament?
4. Name some verses in the Old Testament that are messianic prophecies.
5. If the Bible has predicted the future many times, then who inspired it?
6. Why were many copies of the Old Testament destroyed?
7. In what year were the Dead Sea Scrolls found?

8. Name a book of the Bible found among the Dead Sea Scrolls?
9. When were the books of the New Testament written?
10. How many manuscripts of the New Testament have been found?
11. Which manuscript dates back to about A.D. 130?

Critical Thinking

Looking at the chart on page 26, answer the following questions.

1. How many years were there between the time Herodotus wrote his *History* and the earliest manuscript we have of it?
2. How many more manuscripts are there of the New Testament than of the *Histories* of Tacitus?
3. Homer wrote the *Illiad* in approximately what year?
4. Which book has 9 manuscripts?
5. How much time came between the writing of the New Testament and

the date of the earliest manuscripts
of it?

6. The New Testament was completed by what year?

7. How many more manuscripts of
   the New Testament exist compared with the manuscripts of
   Homer's *Illiad*?

Just For Fun

Make Your Own Scroll

Take two unsharpened pencils, two pieces
of tape, a half-sheet of plain white paper
(without lines). Turn the paper long ways,
roll the paper around each pencil once,
and tape them tightly. Then write a nice
note to your parents or a friend on the inside paper between the two pencils. Roll
the pencils toward the middle, making sure
that the paper is even. Deliver the scroll.
(If you want it to look older, you can soak
it in tea or coffee and let it dry before you
write on it.)

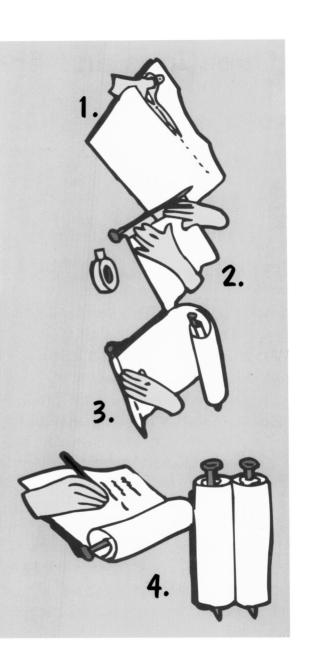

Chapter 7

Which Books Belong in the Bible?

If you have done your Bible homework, then you know that there are 66 different books in the Bible. The Old Testament contains 39 books, and the New Testament contains 27 books. But many books other than these 66 were written during Bible times. Why did some books end up in the Bible, while others did not? Who determined if a book should or should not be in the Bible?

Books of the Old Testament

During Old Testament times, Jews used two rules to determine if a book was from God. First, it had to come from a prophet, or someone to whom God had spoken. Moses, Ezekiel, and Isaiah were well known as prophets. Others—like Daniel, David, and Solomon—were well known as people to whom God had spoken. Any book that did not come from such a person had no chance of ever getting into the Bible.

Second, the writing had to be recognized as coming from God, and had to be used widely by the Israelites. God's people treasured the writings He gave them. Moses wrote God's commandments in

"the book of the Law." Later, Nehemiah began a library, where he put books by prophets. Such writings were precious to the Hebrews. By 425 B.C., the Old Testament books were finished, and by the time Jesus was born, the Jews were using the same 39 books we find in our Old Testament.

Books of the New Testament

The 27 books of the New Testament made their way into the Bible much like the books of the Old Testament. No man, or group of men, decided which books should be included or omitted. Books were included because: (a) they were known to have come from God—they contained the commandments of God; (b) they were written by an apostle or prophet of God —like Peter or Paul; (c) they could be proved to be genuine—such as the book of Luke, written by Luke; (d) they possessed the ability to change people's lives —like Paul's letters; and (e) they were used by Christians.

It was very important to the early Christians to make sure that they trusted only

Sometimes Paul would tell someone else (much like a secretary) what to write in an epistle. But in Colossians 4:18, Paul tells us that He would often sign the letters with his own signature so that people could tell it was from him.

in words that God had inspired. Many people during New Testament times were writing things that did not come from God. Some of these people were trying to say that their writings were just as important as the ones inspired by God. In 2 Thessalonians 2:2, Paul warned the Christians:

"Please don't be so easily shaken and troubled by those who say that the day of the Lord has already begun. Even if they claim to have had a vision, a revelation, or a **letter supposedly from us**, don't believe them" (New Living Translation). Because of such imposters, the Christians were constantly on their guard against fake books. They made sure that they trusted only in God's Word.

Books that don't Belong

Since the apostles and prophets wrote things that were very popular, other people wanted to be like them. These other people wrote books that are not found in the Bible, even though they were written at the same time as books in the Bible. You may hear someone discussing the books found in the Apocrypha (uh-pok-ri-fa—a word that means "hidden" or "concealed"). These books were written between 200 B.C. and A.D. 100.

They are not in the Bible for several reasons. God did not inspire these books. They were not widely recognized by early Christians as being a part of the New Testament. And, the Apocrypha contains "weird" teachings. One book talks about Jesus, as a child, playing with His friends. One boy bumped into Jeus while running, and Jesus killed him! But God's Son would never do that.

God Decides, not Man

Some people think that men chose the books that are in the Bible. They think this because it is a fact that hundreds of years ago, certain groups of men held meetings to vote on the books **they thought** belonged in the Bible. But the truth of the matter is, no book could get into the Bible unless God inspired the book. When the groups of men met to discuss the Bible, they did not have the power to vote some books in and others out. The

councils merely made it clear that they recognized the books God had inspired. God inspired the books of the Bible, and no vote by any council could change that fact.

The Deal is Sealed

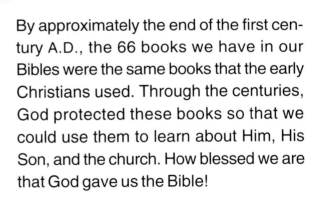

No new books will ever be added to the 66 books found in the Bible that we have today. God has told us that His Word was "once for all delivered to the saints" (Jude 3). God also said that He has given us "all things that pertain to life and godliness" (2 Peter 1:3). No one will ever write a new book that fits into the Bible, because God is finished telling people what to write. He has given us everything we need to know.

By approximately the end of the first century A.D., the 66 books we have in our Bibles were the same books that the early Christians used. Through the centuries, God protected these books so that we could use them to learn about Him, His Son, and the church. How blessed we are that God gave us the Bible!

Chapter 8

What is a Translation?

If you traveled around the world, it would not take you very long to discover that people speak many different languages. In fact, there may be some people at your school or in your Bible class who can speak a different language than you. But this was not always the case. Many years ago, everyone spoke the same language. After the Flood, all of Noah's descendants spoke one language. However, they used this ability to rebel against God. Because of their rebellion, God separated them from each other and gave them many different languages. He did this at a place called the Tower of Babel (the story is told in Genesis 11).

In this world today, there are thousands of different languages. How is it possible for people who speak different languages to communicate with each other? For instance, how can people who speak Spanish communicate with people who speak English? The answer is simple; they must have a translation. A translation is simply bringing over thoughts from one language into another. For example, if you do not know Spanish and someone says to you, "Hola," you will not understand him. Someone must tell you that this means "Hello." That is a translation. The concept of translation is very important when discussing the Bible.

Original Languages of the Old Testament

The Old Testament was written mostly in the Hebrew language. Hebrew writing goes from the right side of the page to the left—exactly the opposite of English. Here is a sample of what Hebrew looks like: דְּהת הוֹלי בךְבלךְ. Can you imagine trying to read the Old Testament in Hebrew? It

33

would be impossible for most of us, since we cannot speak the Hebrew language. For this reason, we need a translation.

Just like the Old Testament, the New Testament was written in a language that is foreign to most of us. It was written almost entirely in Greek. Greek was man's common language during the days of the New Testament, and many people could read and speak Greek. In fact, Greek was such a popular language that the Old Testament was translated from Hebrew into Greek around the year 250 B.C. (this translation was called the Septuagint). Greek more closely resembles English,

because it is written from left to right and some of its letters look similar to English letters. Here is an example of what Greek looks like: προσ ην απ αρχησ. Obviously, most of us would have no idea what the Bible said if we had to read it in Greek.

This Septuagint papyrus of a part of the book of Leviticus is a one of the oldest of its kind in the world.

THREE LANGUAGES, THREE ALPHABETS

For hundreds of years, the people of the Old Testament spoke Hebrew and wrote with an alphabet they borrowed from the Canaanites (similar to the writing shown here).

After a while, the Jews started to speak and write Aramaic. When they made copies of the Old Testament, they kept the Hebrew words but wrote them using their own version of the Aramaic alphabet.

By the time of Jesus, many people in the Roman Empire spoke Greek. Most of the New Testament was written in Greek, but it has some Hebrew and Aramaic words in it, too. In the area where Jesus lived, the people spoke Aramaic as their everyday language.

▷ It might seem weird to speak in one language, and borrow the alphabet of another, but that's just what we do! We speak the English language, but we write down the words using the Latin alphabet.

▷ Jesus and many of His disciples probably were trilingual, which means they could speak or write three languages: the Hebrew of the Old Testament, the Aramaic of the local people, and the Greek of the Roman Empire.

▷ All the alphabets we have talked about so far are related (that is, they all descended from the same ancient alphabet).

▷ Not only do these pictures show three languages and three alphabets, they also show three types of writing materials: stone, parchment (made from animal skin), and papyrus (a paper made from the stems of the papyrus plant or bullrush).

Translations Needed

Most of the first Christians were Jews who could read both Greek and Hebrew. But Christ told His apostles that He wanted the Gospel to spread throughout the whole world. Eventually, the Gospel reached places where the people did not speak Hebrew or Greek. When this happened, translations were needed.

One of the most important translations ever discovered is called "The Old Syriac." Syriac was a major language spoken by many people in Syria and Mesopotamia. When the New Testament came to people who spoke Syriac, they needed to be able to read it in their own language. For this reason, the early Christians translated the Greek Scriptures into Syriac. This happened approximately between A.D. 100-400.

This Syriac translation on vellum is a good example of the Syriac language. It contains about 4 chapters of the book of Romans, and dates back to about A.D. 470

Credit: The Schøyen Collection MS 2530

Another very old and important translation is called "The Old Latin" translation. It was used around A.D. 150, very soon after the New Testament was written. It is special to those of us who speak English, because the first translation of the English Bible was from Latin.

What is a Version?

The best way to translate the Bible would be to read from the original languages in which it was written. However, that did not always happen. Sometimes translators did not have a copy of the Bible in its original languages, or they could not read the original languages. When this happened, they had to make a translation from another translation. For instance, the first Bible that was translated into English was made by reading from a Latin translation. But we have learned that

35

Latin was not the original language of either the Old or the New Testament.

It is here that the term "version" fits into our discussion. A version is a translation of the Bible that was made by reading the Bible in its original language. Any version of the New Testament must come from reading it in Greek. Any version of the Old Testament must come from reading the Old Testament in Hebrew.

Imagine how different our lives would be if God had not allowed the Bible to be translated into other languages. If the Bible could not have been translated, we all would be forced to learn Hebrew and Greek in order to read the Holy Book. Thank God that we all can read a copy of the Bible in our own language.

HOW WE GOT OUR ENGLISH BIBLE

Old Testament (Hebrew)
finished by 400 B.C.

New Testament (Greek)
finished by A.D. 100

Scrolls transferred to
sheets of papyrus
2nd century A.D.

Latin Vulgate
around
A.D. 400

FIRST COMPLETE BIBLE IN ENGLISH

Wycliffe's Bible
1384

FIRST PRINTED BOOK

Gutenberg Bible
1455

Erasmus' Greek New Testament
1516

Tyndale's New Testament
1526

FIRST COMPLETE PRINTED BIBLE IN ENGLISH

Coverdale's Bible
1535

Matthew's Bible
1537

Great Bible
1539

Bishops' Bible
1568

King James Bible
1611

Most English Bibles of this time
were revisions of previous translations,
but were checked against an ever-
improving supply of Greek and
Hebrew texts.

Most modern Bible translations are
made directly from the Hebrew
and Greek texts.

Chapter 9

Are There Mistakes in the Bible?

Maybe you have played the game called "Gossip." It is a very easy game. Several people get in a circle or a straight line. The person at the beginning of the circle or line thinks of a sentence like "the red horse fell into the water." That person whispers the sentence into the ear of the person next to him. He cannot repeat the sentence after it has been whispered, and he must talk

very softly. The next person in line listens carefully and then whispers the sentence she heard into the ear of the person next to her. After the sentence has gone through every person in the line or circle, the last person repeats the sentence that he was told. Most every time, the sentence at the end of the game is not the same one that was whispered at the beginning. For instance, the last person in the line might have heard something like "the dead horse turned into the otter" instead of the real sentence, "the red horse fell into the water." The game does a good job of showing that words

and sentences can get confused when they are passed from one person to another.

Hold on just one second! Hasn't the Bible been passed down through many generations, copied thousands of times, and translated into many different languages? Does that mean that its message has been altered like the sentence in the game described? In fact, some people claim that the Bible has over 300,000 mistakes in its text. Is that true?

Please, Copy Correctly

As we have discussed in earlier chapters, there are over 5,000 ancient copies of the different New Testament writings. The original books and letters that were written by the apostles were inspired by God, and had absolutely no errors in them. However, when other people who were not inspired by God began to copy the books of the Bible, they sometimes made mistakes during copying. For instance, they might have been trying to copy the word "late" and accidentally wrote down "later." Most of the mistakes were very small and occurred by accident. But some of the

mistakes were big, and sometimes were made on purpose. Because of these "copyists' mistakes," some of the ancient copies of the Bible look a little bit different from each other. So how do we know which one is the right one and which one has the mistake.

Comparing Copies

In almost every case, it is very easy to see what the inspired writer really said. Even though some of the copies may have mistakes in them, when all the copies are placed side by side and compared to one another, the original message can be seen quite clearly. See the chart above for an example.

As we look at these sentences, it is not difficult to see that the original sentence said "John's best friend loves to read books about the Bible." Just because some of the sentences have mistakes (also called variations) in them, the original message was not altered. Those people who say that the Bible contains over 300,000 errors count every single spelling and grammar mistake in each different copy. They would say that the sentence about John

Let me show you how this works. Several copies of a sentence have been listed below. Try to decide which one is the original sentence.

John's best friend loves to read books about the Bible.

Johns best friend loves to read books about the Bible.

John's best friends loves to read books about the Bible.

John's best frind loves to read books about the Bibl.

John's best friend lives to read books about the Bible.

John's friend likes to read books about Bible.

has 9 mistakes. But really, it has no mistakes in it, because the original sentence has been perfectly preserved, even though some of the copies contain mistakes.

Small Stuff

Also, it is important for you to know that most of the variations in ancient copies of the Bible deal with tiny words like "a" or "the." For instance, one copy might say something like, "the disciples went to **a** house," while another ancient copy might say "the disciples went to **the** house." The meaning of the text is not altered by these tiny variations in the text. We know exactly what the original document was saying.

Another kind of "little" copy mistake happened when writing down names. For example, the original document might have used the name "Jonah," but when the copyist wrote the name, he spelled it "Jona." The meaning of the name was not changed and neither was our understanding of the person under discussion. This situation sometimes occurred with names of cities and towns. But even though copyists occasionally altered a few letters in the name of a person or a town, so small were the changes that the proper person or place still could be identified.

We Have the Right One

After all ancient copies of the Bible are compared, it is obvious that we have well over 99% of the original text that God inspired the writers to record. Of the remaining tiny part that we are not exactly sure about, none of it deals with one thing that would change a single item of faith. Many people have accused the Bible of being filled with thousands of mistakes made by copyists and translators. However, when all of the copies are placed side by side and compared to one another, the final product is more accurate than any ancient book ever produced. When you pick up the Bible, you can know for sure

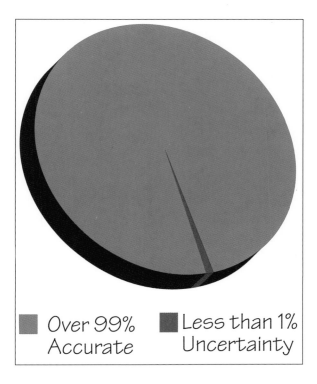

Over 99% Accurate — Less than 1% Uncertainty

that you are holding in your hand the words that the inspired writers wrote down thousands of years ago.

Questions and Activities Chapters 7-9

Vocabulary

Apocrypha   Septuagint
Translation   Version
Hebrew   Greek

Critical Thinking

In each set of sentences, find the original message. As you are working, attempt to count the number of variations.

a. How blissed we are that God give us the Bible!
b. How blesed we are that God gave us the Bible!
c. How blested we are that God gave us the Bble!
d. How blessed we are that God gave us the Bible!
e. How blessed we are that God gave us the Bible
f. How blessed we our that God gave us the Bib
g. ow blessed we are that God give us the Bi

Review

1. How many books are in the Old Testament?
2. The New Testament contains how many books?
3. How many books are in the entire Bible?
4. What year were the Old Testament books finished?
5. What happened at the Tower of Babel?
6. The Old Testament was originally written in what language?
7. The New Testament was originally written in what language?
8. What is a variation?
9. What year was the Septuagint created?
10. Name two important ancient translations.

The Gossip Game

Play the game "Gossip" (described in chapter 9) with some friends or family. How difficult is it to accurately pass information from person to person? Why do you think the Bible is so accurate, even after it has been "passed down" through many generations?

Chapter 10

The Old Testament

Almost all of us have been shopping in a big grocery store at one time or another. Sometimes, it is not very easy to find the things that we need. Grocery stores are big, they have several different aisles, and many of the aisles look the same. But once we understand how the grocery store is arranged, it is much easier to find what we need. For instance, suppose your mother sends you on an errand to find some milk. Since you know that milk must stay cold in order to be good, you simply go to the section of the grocery store (usually in the back) where the refrigerated coolers are. All the things that must stay cool such as milk, cheese, and cookie dough can be found in the refrigerated sections. Knowing this kind of infor-

mation helps us find all the things we need in the grocery store.

The Bible is similar to a big grocery store. It is composed of different books that look similar to one another and can sometimes be confusing. However, once we understand how the Bible is arranged, then we can find things in it much easier —just like in the grocery store.

The Two Biggest Parts

The Bible is divided into two major parts —the Old Testament and the New Testament. The word "testament" means a covenant or agreement. Therefore, the Old Testament was God's old agreement with mankind and the New Testament is God's new agreement or covenant with mankind.

The Old Testament

There are 39 books in the Old Testament. The original Old Testament docu-

ments were written mostly in the Hebrew language. Moses wrote the first five books of the Old Testament in approximately 1500 B.C. Malachi, the last book in the Old Testament, was written around 450 B.C.

The 39 books of the Old Testament are divided into five sections:

[1] The books of the law—Genesis, Exodus, Leviticus, Numbers, and Deuteronomy. These books are known as the books of the law because they explain how God picked the Jews to be His special people and then gave them the Old Law, including the Ten Commandments. God inspired Moses to write these five books.

[2] The books of history—Joshua, Judges, Ruth, 1&2 Samuel, 1&2 Kings, 1&2 Chronicles, Ezra, Nehemiah, and Esther. The 12 books of history record the history of the Israelites after they had received the Law. These Old Testament books record the actions of the Israelites in much the same way as our modern history books record the history of the United States—including wars, treaties, and the names of important leaders. The 12 books of history show us how kind and forgiv-

ing God was, even when the Jews and their leaders refused to worship Him properly.

[3] The books of Poetry—Job, Psalms, Proverbs, Ecclesiastes, and Song of Solomon. Roses are red, violets are blue, every nation in the world writes poetry, too. The 5 books of Old Testament poetry contain beautiful poetry. The reason they may not look like the poetry we know is because they were written in the Hebrew language. When poetry is translated from one language into another, it loses some of its rhyme and verse. Psalms is a book of poetry filled with catchy songs that the Jews could easily memorize and teach their children. Proverbs is a book filled with very short quotes that could be used in almost any part of everyday life. If you could read Hebrew, then you would see that the poetry in these books is beautiful and very memorable.

Nehemiah, an Old Testament book of history, tells about a man named Nehemiah who rebuilt the walls of Jerusalem.

[4] The books of the Major Prophets—Isaiah, Jeremiah, Lamentations, Ezekiel, and Daniel. During the history of the Jewish nation, God set some men apart from others to preach His message to the people. These men were very special men who listened to God, and only preached the messages that God told them. They were called prophets. The prophets not only could preach, but also could predict what was going to happen in the future.

And some of the prophets could even perform miracles like raising people from the dead. The prophets were some of God's most powerful messengers on the Earth. However, most of the time the Jews did not listen to the prophets. In fact, many of the prophets were killed and chased away from their homes. Being a prophet was dangerous work, but the men who preached faithfully were always remembered by God for their loyal service.

[5] The Minor Prophets—Hosea, Joel, Amos, Obadiah, Jonah, Micah, Nahum, Habakkuk, Zephaniah, Haggai, Zechariah, and Malachi. The Minor Prophets wrote just like the Major Prophets. They are not divided because one group was better or more important than the other group. They are divided into two groups because the Major Prophets wrote long books, while the Minor Prophets wrote books that are much shorter. That is really the only thing that separates the Major Prophets from the Minor Prophets.

Finding What You Need

Now that you know how the Old Testament is arranged, it will be much easier for you to find what you are looking for. For example, where would you go if you wanted to find the Ten Commandments? You would look in one of the first five books known as the books of law, since the Ten Commandments were part of the Old Law. Again, where would you look for memorable songs and short quotes? Right again —the books of poetry. And where would you expect to find writings that could predict the future? Yes—the Major and Minor prophets.

Learning these different sections of the Old Testament makes it easier for you to understand the Bible. And this information will help you find things in the Old Testament much faster. We should thank God that the Bible is arranged so that we can understand it.

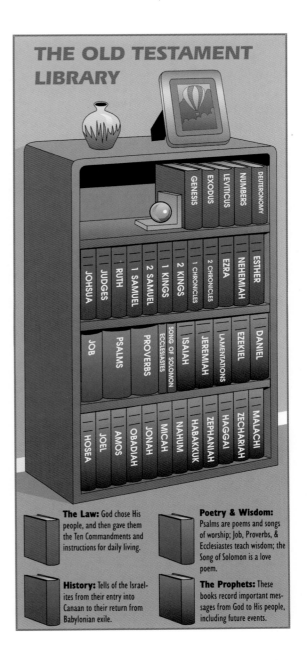

THE OLD TESTAMENT LIBRARY

GENESIS EXODUS LEVITICUS NUMBERS DEUTERONOMY

JOHSUA JUDGES RUTH 1 SAMUEL 2 SAMUEL 1 KINGS 2 KINGS 1 CHRONICLES 2 CHRONICLES EZRA NEHEMIAH ESTHER

JOB PSALMS PROVERBS ECCLESIASTES SONG OF SOLOMON ISAIAH JEREMIAH LAMENTATIONS EZEKIEL DANIEL

HOSEA JOEL AMOS OBADIAH JONAH MICAH NAHUM HABAKKUK ZEPHANIAH HAGGAI ZECHARIAH MALACHI

The Law: God chose His people, and then gave them the Ten Commandments and instructions for daily living.

History: Tells of the Israelites from their entry into Canaan to their return from Babylonian exile.

Poetry & Wisdom: Psalms are poems and songs of worship; Job, Proverbs, & Ecclesiastes teach wisdom; the Song of Solomon is a love poem.

The Prophets: These books record important messages from God to His people, including future events.

Chapter 11

The New Testament

The Old Testament was written mainly for the Jewish people to obey thousands of years ago. It tells us amazing stories about huge giants, man-eating fish, and strong men who could kill lions with their bare hands. However, even though the Old Testament shows us about God and how He dealt with man, it cannot show us what we are supposed to do today in order to follow God.

When Jesus Christ died on the cross, He did away with the Old Law that is found in the Old Testament, and He made a New Law that is found only in the New Testament. Today, the New Testament is the place to go in order to find out what our God wants us to do. And, as we learned in the last chapter, if we want to be able to understand the New Testament, then we need to understand how it is arranged.

The Arrangement of the New Testament

There are 27 books in the New Testament. Matthew is the first, and Revelation is the last. These 27 books are divided into 4 major parts.

The Gospels. The word gospel means "good news." The first four books of the New Testament are Matthew, Mark, Luke, and John. They are known as the gospels because they tell the story of Jesus' life, death, and resurrection. Since the story of Jesus is good news for a sinful world, it is known as the Gospel.

History. This section of the New Testament has only one book—Acts. Acts was written by Luke, and tells the history of the apostles. After Jesus returned to heaven at the end of the gospels, His followers went all over the world preaching the good news of His life, death, and resurrection. Because of their preaching,

Acts, the book of history in the New Testament, tells how the Apostle Paul had to be lowered in a basket to avoid being captured (Acts 9:25).

preached the Gospel throughout the world, many churches were started in different cities. The apostles and other writers needed a way to explain to these churches how to worship and how to live. So they wrote letters to these churches. For instance, the book of Romans is a letter written to the church at Rome, and the book of Ephesians is an epistle written to the church in Ephesus. Sometimes these epistles were written to an individual person (like 1 and 2 Timothy, which

God's Word spread throughout the whole world, and the church that Jesus promised to build (Matthew 16:18) spread along with the Word. The book of Acts tells about the spread of the church and about many brave things that Christ's disciples did in order to preach the Gospel to every nation.

The Epistles. "Epistle" is another word for a personal letter. When the apostles are letters written by the apostle Paul to his helper named Timothy). The epistles were written to people who were already Christians, yet who needed some encouragement, an answer to a question, or spiritual discipline. The epistles start with Romans and go through the book of Jude.

Prophecy. This section has only one book—Revelation. The reason it is called a prophetic book is because it told the people in the first century things that were going to happen to them in the future. Most of the things discussed in Revelation have already occurred. Unfortunately, some people misuse the book to try to predict the end of time, which is something the book was not intended to do. It is important to remember when reading the book of Revelation that it uses lots of symbolic language, and nothing in it goes against the rest of the Bible.

The New Testament was completed about 500 years after Malachi. However, the New Testament picks up right where the Old Testament left off. All of the prophets had been telling about the coming Messiah Who would save the world and establish a spiritual kingdom. The entire Jewish nation was waiting for the Messiah. The four gospels tell the story of Jesus, and prove by His miracles and teachings that He was the coming Messiah.

The rest of the New Testament outlines the new covenant that Jesus established. No longer would people offer animal sacrifices of bulls and goats to receive forgiveness of their sins as they did in the Old Testament. Under Jesus' new covenant, His own death on the cross would be the only sacrifice that could forgive sins. It is very

important to understand that the new covenant (New Testament) took the place of the old covenant (Old Testament). Hebrews 8:13 says: "In that He says, 'a new covenant,' He has made the first obsolete. Now what is becoming obsolete and growing old is ready to vanish away." The Old Testament is a wonderful set of books that can teach people today many amazing things about God. In fact, the Old Testament prepared the world for Jesus, the coming Messiah. But after Jesus lived, died, and rose again, God created a new system and made a new covenant (agreement) with mankind. The details of that new agreement are found in the New Testament—the only place mankind can go to find salvation.

Each book of the Bible complements the others in a single, unified plan. From Genesis to Revelation there is a marvelous unfolding of the general theme of man's fall, God's plan for his salvation, the sinless life and atoning death of Jesus Christ, and the ultimate victory of the Christian system. In essence, the Bible is the story of one problem—sin—with one solution, Jesus Christ.

THE NEW TESTAMENT LIBRARY

MATTHEW
MARK
LUKE
JOHN

ACTS
ROMANS
1 CORINTHIANS
2 CORINTHIANS
GALATIANS
EPHESIANS
PHILIPPIANS
COLOSSIANS
1 THESSALONIANS
2 THESSALONIANS

1 TIMOTHY
2 TIMOTHY
TITUS
PHILEMON
HEBREWS
JAMES
1 PETER
2 PETER
1 JOHN
2 JOHN
3 JOHN
JUDE
REVELATION

The Gospels: "Gospel" means "good news," as in the Good News of salvation that Jesus preached. Each book tells the story of Jesus' life in a slightly different way.

Epistles: These letters were addressed to either a group (such as the Christians in Rome) or to a person (such as Titus).

History: The book of Acts gives us a history of the early church. It tells us what the apostles did to spread the Good News.

Prophecy: The book of Revelation contains visions given by Christ to the apostle John. It told Christians what to expect in the near future.

Chapter 12

Does the Bible Lie?

The light shone brightly into the eyes of the suspect who was seated between two FBI special agents in black suits. "Where were you the night of October 31, 2004?" demanded one of the agents. The suspect nervously muttered, "I already told you, I was at a Halloween party with some friends." The questioning continued: "And what exactly were you doing at that party?" asked the same demanding agent. "I bobbed for apples," retorted the suspect in his shaky voice. Many hours later, during a different questioning period, another officer asked the same suspect a question that seemed to be very silly: "Have you ever bobbed for apples?" The suspect firmly replied, "No, I have never in my life bobbed for apples."

Obviously, the suspect had lied. He could not truthfully say in one breath that he bobbed for apples, and then in the next breath say that he never bobbed for apples in all his life. Either he had or he had not bobbed for apples; both his statements could not have been true.

Some people accuse the Bible of doing the exact same thing as the lying suspect. They claim that the Bible contradicts itself, which means that it says one thing in one place, and then says something totally opposite in another place.

The Christian claims that the Bible is the Word of God. Yet if it contradicts itself, then that would make God a liar. And since the Bible says that God cannot lie (Titus 1:2), then any book with contradictions in it could not have been inspired by God.

Therefore, if a real contradiction can be found anywhere in the Bible, then it is not the Word of God.

The truth is, when all the facts are considered, each thing that people have found in the Bible that they thought was a contradiction has been shown to be something other than a true mistake. That is a powerful statement, considering the fact that no book in the world has been examined more closely than the Bible.

Good Rules to Follow

Generally, most of the things that people think are mistakes in the Bible can be solved by answering three simple questions: (1) Is the same person or thing being considered?; (2) Is the same time period being discussed?; and (3) Is the same sense under consideration?

Think with me. Suppose that someone says, "Leroy Jones is rich," and "Leroy Jones is poor." Do those two statements contradict (go against) each other? Not necessarily. Many people are named Leroy Jones (O.K., maybe not all that many, but at least two). It could be that the Leroy Jones in Florida is rich, but the Leroy Jones in New York is poor. The same person or thing must be under consideration.

L.J. in Florida   L.J. in New York

Further, the same time period must be under consideration. Leroy Jones could have made a fortune in his early twenties as an oil tycoon and been very rich, but after a terrible stock market crash could have lost everything he owned. At one time, then, he was rich, but now he is poor. The two statements could have been accurately describing his life at the time each was made.

Young L.J.   Old L.J.

Also, the statements must be talking about the same sense. Leroy Jones could have more money than anyone else in the entire world, but if he is not following God, then he is poor. On the other hand, he could have absolutely no money, but be rich in spiritual blessings. After all, "Has God not chosen the poor of this world to be rich in faith" (James 2:5)? Answering these three questions helps tremendously in resolving the contradiction controversy.

L.J. is poor in the world's eyes		L.J. is rich in God's sight

Adding Information to a Story

Sometimes, people accuse the Bible of making mistakes when the same story is told differently by different authors. For example, in Matthew 14:21 the Bible says that Jesus fed about five thousand men, and that He also fed women and children. But in Mark 6:44, it says that He fed about five thousand men. Mark never mentions the women and children. Is that a mistake? No, of course not. Did He feed about 5,000 men? Yes, and that makes Mark correct. Did Jesus feed about 5,000 men, along with some women and children? Yes, which makes Matthew right, too. Just because one account "adds" some things does not mean that the accounts contradict each other.

To illustrate this point, suppose you and your mother went to the mall. When you came home, your sister asked what you did at the mall. You told her about play-

ing video games and eating cinnamon rolls. Your mother told her about all the good clothing stores you visited. Your mother's details are different from yours, but they are not contradictory. She simply "added" some things to your story.

Everyday Conversation

Suppose that the weatherman comes on the television and announces, "the Sun will rise at 6:03 a.m. on Saturday." Even though the Earth rotates and the Sun really is not rising at all, we have no problem understanding his comment. We call this "phenomenal" language—language that is used in everyday speech to refer to ordinary phenomena.

On occasion, the Bible also uses this type of language. In Psalm 50:1, the writer described the Sun as rising, and in 1 Corinthians 15:6 Paul described some of the Christians who had died as having "fallen asleep." No one would accuse the weatherman of making a scientific mistake when he says that the Sun will rise. Likewise, the Bible should not be accused of mak-

ing mistakes when it uses the same type of language.

No one has ever found one real contradiction in the Bible. Isn't it wonderful that God has given us the Bible without any contradictions in it?

Chapter 13

Counting the Cost

Almost 3,500 years ago, God began the process of bringing the Bible down to us through many generations of people so that we could have a Bible to read in our own language.

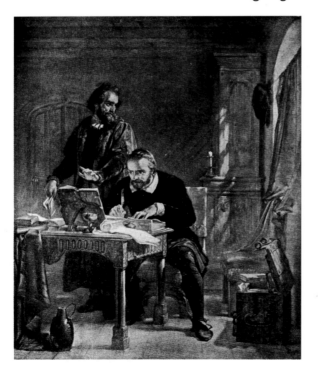

He safely guarded the Bible from errors for those thousands of years, and He made sure that the Bible was written and arranged in a way that ordinary people like us can understand. So, how much did it cost to get the Bible from God to you? No one can give an amount in money, because there is not enough money in the world to cover the cost. But when we look back at the history of some of the people who were a part of the process, we can see that it cost some of them their lives.

William Tyndale

One such man was named William Tyndale. He was born around the year 1495 in England. He grew up with the desire to be a priest, but he soon learned that the religious system in his church was cruel and unfair. In fact, the most precious document the church possessed, the

Bible, was rarely even translated into English, the common man's language. Instead, the Bible was written in Latin and used only by the priests (very few of the common people could read Latin). The priests thought that the common people could not understand the Bible, so they certainly did not need one in a language that they could read.

But William Tyndale disagreed with this idea. He thought that everyone deserved to have a chance to read the Bible. His dream was to translate and print the Bible in English so that ordinary people could read it. He told this dream to one of the priests and the priest greatly discouraged the idea. Tyndale was upset, and he told that priest: "If God spares my life, I will cause the boy that drives the plow to know more scripture than you do." That was his dream—for a plowboy to know just as much scripture as the priest. But that dream would not come without effort.

Henry the VIII was the king of England at the time, and he did not want the Bible translated into English. He did not want his subjects to know the Bible, so he

King Henry VIII

sought to arrest Tyndale. Tyndale ran for his life, and escaped to Germany where he lived in exile, poverty, persecution, and pain. Yet he never stopped his tireless work on the English translation of the Scriptures. In 1525, he completed his copy of the New Testament and printed 18,000 copies, smuggling them into England. The Bishop of London discovered that the Bibles were coming into England and purchased an entire shipment of the Bibles.

The bishop took these Bible and burned them in a public place for everyone to see. What the bishop did not realize was that the money he used to purchase the shipment provided the funds for the publication of the second edition of Tyndale's English translation.

Henry the VIII was extremely angry, and demanded that William Tyndale be put to death. Yet Tyndale had become good at hiding, and no one could catch him. But in 1534, Tyndale met a man named Henry Phillips who pretended to admire and respect Tyndale's cause. He invited William over for dinner. Poor William Tyndale did not know that Henry Phillips was working for the king of England, or that the dinner invitation was a trap. When Tyndale arrived, he was captured and handed over to the English authorities.

Tyndale was imprisoned for 6 months and treated terribly. Finally, he was sentenced to be strangled and burned at the stake. His final words before he died were: "Lord, open the king of England's eyes." Within

a year of his death, the king's eyes were opened. Henry the VIII gave the English translation royal recognition and sent one to each town.

Conclusion

As you can see, it has cost a lot to get the Bible to us. Throughout the ages, men and women from many different time periods and many different countries have put their lives in danger so that you and I can read the Bible in our own language. We have seen how the Bible started out on materials such as stone tablets and scrolls of papyrus. It was originally written mostly in Hebrew and Greek—languages that very few of us who speak English can understand. Yet careful scribes copied and translated the Bible so that it could be passed from one generation to the next. Many of these ancient copies have been preserved until now, and we can compare them to ensure that we have the words of the inspired writers. Each book in the Bible has been carefully examined to make sure that it was inspired by God, rather than being written by an uninspired person. Without a doubt, the Bible that we have today is the Word of God.

Sadly, many people do not read the Bible, even though they understand that it is the Word of God. Many people own Bibles, but lots of times those Bibles just sit on a shelf and collect dust. In some homes, the Bible gets less attention than TV or video games. How sad it must make God to know that He went through all the trouble to preserve His Word so that people could read and understand it, yet many of those people do not want to do so.

God loves every person in the world. His Son, Jesus Christ, died to prove that love to the world. The wonderful story of that love is found only in the Bible. God loved us enough to make sure that we have the Bible. Will we love Him enough to study it?

Questions and Activities Chapters 10-13

Vocabulary

Testament   Gospel
Epistle   Contradict
Covenant   Prophet
Phenomenal language

Review

1. Name the two major sections of the Bible.
2. Name the five sections of the Old Testament.
3. What are the four main sections of the New Testament?
4. Why are some of the books of prophecy in the Old Testament called Major, while others are called Minor?
5. Who did God inspire to write the first five books of the Old Testament?
6. Which book is filled with catchy songs that the Israelites could have taught their children?
7. Which section of the Bible has the rules for how we should live today?
8. What four books make up the gospels?
9. Which book in the New Testament is a book of prophecy?
10. What was the book of Revelation **not** intended to do?
11. The Bible is a story of one big problem. What is it?
12. What is the solution to the one problem discussed in the Bible?
13. Does the Bible ever contradict itself?
14. What was William Tyndale's dream?
15. What is the last book in the New Testament?
16. About how many men did God use to write the Bible?
17. What is an epistle?
18. When Christ died on the cross, what did He do away with?

Critical Thinking

Read each Bible reference and use one of the rules in chapter 12 to find a solution. Tell which rule you use.

1. a. Job has lots of money, cattle, and good health (Job 1:3).
    b. Job has no earthly riches and is in very bad health (Job 1:13-20; 2:8).
2. a. "Then God saw everything that He had made, and indeed it was very good" (Genesis 1:31).
    b. "Then the Lord saw that the wickedness of man was great in the earth, and that every intent of the thoughts of his heart was only evil continually" (Genesis 6:5).
3. a. "The length of the ark shall be three hundred cubits, its width fifty cubits, and its height thirty cubits" (Genesis 6:15).
    b. "And they shall make an ark of acacia wood; two and a half cubits shall be its length, a cubit and a half its width, and a cubit and a half its height" (Exodus 25:10).
4. How has God chosen the poor of this world to be rich (James 2:5)?
5. How has God chosen the wisdom of this world to be foolishness (1 Corinthians 1:26)?

Just For Fun

Sword Drill

Have a teacher or parent call out random verses in the Bible and race your friends or classmate to see who can get to the verse first. Whoever holds his or her hand up first and reads the correct verse, scores a point. Whoever speaks without being called, loses a point. The person who has the most points at the end of the drill wins. (HINT: Knowing the books of the Bible in order will help you.)

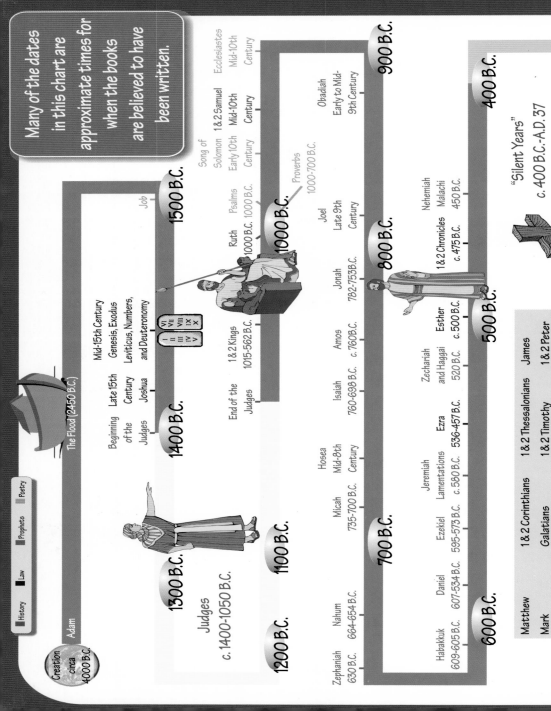

Timeline for the Books of the Bible

Many of the dates in this chart are approximate times for when the books are believed to have been written.

Legend: History · Law · Prophets · Poetry

Creation circa 4000 B.C.

Adam

The Flood (2450 B.C.)

1500 B.C.
Job

1400 B.C.
Mid-15th Century — Genesis, Exodus, Leviticus, Numbers, and Deuteronomy
Late 15th Century — Joshua
Beginning of the Judges
End of the Judges

1300 B.C.
Judges c. 1400-1050 B.C.

1200 B.C.

1100 B.C.

1000 B.C.
Ruth 1000 B.C.
Psalms 1000 B.C.
Song of Solomon Early 10th Century
1 & 2 Samuel Mid-10th Century
Ecclesiastes Mid-9th Century
Proverbs 1000-700 B.C.

900 B.C.
Obadiah Early to Mid-9th Century
1 & 2 Kings 1015-562 B.C.
Joel Late 9th Century

800 B.C.
Jonah 782-753 B.C.
Amos c. 760 B.C.
Isaiah 760-698 B.C.
Hosea Mid-8th Century
Micah 735-700 B.C.

700 B.C.
Jeremiah
Lamentations c. 560 B.C.
Nahum 664-654 B.C.

600 B.C.
Zephaniah 630 B.C.
Habakkuk 609-605 B.C.
Daniel 607-534 B.C.
Ezekiel 595-573 B.C.

500 B.C.
Ezra 536-457 B.C.
Zechariah and Haggai 520 B.C.
Esther c. 500 B.C.
Nehemiah
1 & 2 Chronicles c. 475 B.C.
Malachi 450 B.C.

400 B.C.
"Silent Years" c. 400 B.C.-A.D. 37

A.D. 37

A.D. 100
Matthew
Mark
Luke
John
Acts
Romans
1 & 2 Corinthians
Galatians
Ephesians
Phillippians
Colossians
1 & 2 Thessalonians
1 & 2 Timothy
Titus
Philemon
Hebrews
James
1 & 2 Peter
1, 2 & 3 John
Jude
Revelation

c. = circa, which means "approximately"